The Rise Of Zlatan Ibrahimovic

Table of contents

Chapter 1
Introduction

Zlatan Ibrahimovic, the Swedish football superstar, is a name that resonates with football fans all over the world. Known for his incredible skill, strength, and personality on and off the pitch, Ibrahimovic has carved out a legendary career spanning over two decades. His rise to fame has been nothing short of remarkable, with his journey taking him from humble beginnings in Sweden to the pinnacle of football success. In this article, we will explore the rise of Zlatan Ibrahimovic, delving into his early life, career highlights, and impact on the sport. From his time at Ajax to his recent return to AC Milan, we will examine how Ibrahimovic has become one of the most iconic figures in modern football. So, sit back and join us as we take a journey through the life and times of Zlatan Ibrahimovic.

Chapter 2
Early Life and Career

Zlatan Ibrahimovic was born on October 3, 1981, in Malmo, Sweden. His parents were immigrants from the former Yugoslavia, with his father being a Bosniak Muslim from Bosnia and Herzegovina and his mother being a Croat Catholic from Croatia. Growing up in a tough neighborhood, Ibrahimovic was exposed to the harsh realities of life at an early age. However, he found solace in football, which he began playing at the age of six.

Ibrahimovic's talent on the pitch was evident from a young age, and he quickly caught the attention of local clubs. At the age of 15, he joined the youth academy of Malmo FF, one of the most successful clubs in Sweden. He made his professional debut for the club in 1999, at the age of 17, and quickly established himself as one of their key players.

In 2001, Ibrahimovic was signed by Dutch giants Ajax Amsterdam, where he played alongside future stars such as Rafael van der Vaart and Wesley Sneijder. He helped Ajax win two Eredivisie titles and was named Dutch Footballer of the Year in 2004. His performances caught the attention of some of Europe's biggest clubs, and in 2004 he was signed by Italian giants Juventus.

Ibrahimovic's time at Juventus was a huge success, as he helped the club win two Serie A titles. However, his time at the club was marred by controversy, as Juventus were later stripped of their titles due to their involvement in a match-fixing scandal. Ibrahimovic then moved to Inter Milan, where he continued to dominate Italian football, winning three more Serie A titles and being named Serie A Footballer of the Year in 2008.

In 2009, Ibrahimovic made a big-money move to Spanish giants Barcelona, where he played alongside superstars such as Lionel Messi and Xavi. However, his time at the club was short-lived, as he struggled to adapt to the team's playing style and clashed with then-manager Pep Guardiola. He then moved to AC Milan on loan, where he rediscovered his form and helped the club win the Serie A title in

2011.

Ibrahimovic has since played for several other top clubs, including Paris Saint-Germain, Manchester United, and LA Galaxy. In January 2020, he returned to AC Milan on a six-month contract, and has since extended his stay with the club. Despite being in his late 30s, Ibrahimovic continues to be one of the most dominant players in world football, and his impact on the sport will be felt for years to come.

Chapter 3
Move To Ajax

At the age of 19, Ibrahimovic was scouted by Ajax Amsterdam and was offered a trial at the club. Despite initially struggling to adapt to the Dutch style of play, he impressed the coaches with his technical ability and physical prowess. He was eventually signed by the club in 2001 for a fee of €8.7 million.

Ibrahimovic's first season at Ajax was a difficult one, as he struggled to establish himself in the team and was often criticized by fans and media. However, he persevered and gradually began to find his form, scoring his first goal for the club in a match against FC Groningen.

In his second season at Ajax, Ibrahimovic established himself as one of the team's key players, scoring 13 goals in 25 league appearances. He helped the club win the Eredivisie title and was named Dutch Footballer of the Year.

Over the next two seasons, Ibrahimovic continued to impress at Ajax, scoring a total of 35 goals in 74 league appearances. He helped the club win another Eredivisie title in 2004 and was named Dutch Footballer of the Year for the second time.

Ibrahimovic's performances at Ajax caught the attention of some of Europe's biggest clubs, and he was eventually signed by Italian giants Juventus in 2004. However, his time at Ajax will always be remembered as the place where he first made a name for himself on the European stage.

Chapter 4
Success At Juventus

At Juventus, Ibrahimovic continued to showcase his talent and became a key player for the team. In his first season, he scored 16 goals in 35 league appearances, helping the club win the Serie A title. He also scored a crucial goal in the UEFA Champions League quarter-finals against Werder Bremen.

In the following season, Ibrahimovic scored 15 goals in 32 league appearances as Juventus finished second in the Serie A. He also helped the club reach the knockout stages of the Champions League, scoring two goals in the group stage.

Ibrahimovic's impressive performances at Juventus earned him a move to Inter Milan in 2006, where he continued to establish himself as one of the best strikers in Europe. However, his time at Juventus was a crucial period in his career, where he developed his skills and became a champion.

Chapter 5
Controversial Inter Milan Spell

During his time at Inter Milan, Ibrahimovic was involved in several controversial incidents, both on and off the pitch. In one match against Fiorentina, he was accused of intentionally elbowing an opponent, which resulted in a three-match ban. He was also involved in a heated argument with teammate Patrick Vieira during a training session.

Off the pitch, Ibrahimovic was criticized for his behavior towards fans and the media. He once famously said, "I don't give a damn about the critics. I am the best in the world, and that's all there is to it." This attitude did not endear him to many people, and he was often seen as arrogant and difficult to work with.

Despite these controversies, Ibrahimovic continued to score goals and help Inter Milan win titles. In his first season with the club, he scored 17 goals in 26 league appearances, helping them win the Serie A title. He also helped them reach the quarter-finals of the Champions League.

In his second season, Ibrahimovic scored 25 goals in 35 league appearances as Inter Milan won another Serie A title. He was also named the Serie A Footballer of the Year for the second consecutive season.

Overall, Ibrahimovic's time at Inter

Milan was successful on the pitch, but marred by controversy off it.

Chapter 6
Dominant Period At Ac Milan

During his time at AC Milan, Ibrahimovic had one of the most dominant periods of his career. He joined the club on loan in 2010 and quickly became a fan favorite with his impressive performances on the pitch and his charismatic personality off it.

In his first season with the club, Ibrahimovic scored 14 goals in 29 league appearances, helping AC Milan win the Serie A title. He also scored two goals in the team's 3-0 victory over Juventus in the Italian Super Cup final.

The following season, Ibrahimovic

continued to impress, scoring 28 goals in 32 league appearances as AC Milan finished second in Serie A. He also helped the team reach the quarter-finals of the Champions League, scoring four goals in eight appearances.

In his third and final season with the club, Ibrahimovic scored 10 goals in 18 league appearances before suffering a season-ending injury. Despite his absence, AC Milan went on to win the Serie A title.

Throughout his time at AC Milan, Ibrahimovic was known for his leadership on and off the pitch. He was often seen mentoring younger players and pushing his teammates to perform at their best. His dominant performances and charismatic personality made him a beloved figure among AC Milan fans.

Chapter 7
Move To Paris saint-Germain

After his successful stint at AC Milan, Ibrahimovic moved to Paris Saint-Germain (PSG) in 2012. He quickly established himself as a key player for the club, scoring 30 goals in his first season and helping PSG win the Ligue 1 title.

In the following seasons, Ibrahimovic continued to dominate in the French league, scoring 26, 19, and 38 goals respectively in the next three seasons. He also helped PSG win several domestic trophies, including the Coupe de France and the Coupe de la Ligue.

Ibrahimovic's performances for PSG earned him numerous individual awards, including four consecutive Ligue 1 Player of the Year awards. He also became the club's all-time leading scorer with 156 goals in 180 appearances.

Off the pitch, Ibrahimovic was known for his outspoken personality and his confidence in his abilities. He often made headlines with his controversial statements and his larger-than-life persona.

Overall, Ibrahimovic's time at PSG cemented his status as one of the greatest footballers of his generation. His dominant performances and charismatic personality made him a fan favorite at the club and earned him a place in PSG's history books.

Chapter 8
Move To Manchester United

After a successful stint at PSG, Ibrahimovic moved to Manchester United in 2016. He quickly re-established himself as a key player for the club, scoring 28 goals in his first season and helping United win the Europa League and the League Cup.

However, Ibrahimovic suffered a serious knee injury towards the end of the season, which kept him out of action for several months. Despite this setback, he signed a new one-year contract with United for the 2017-18 season.

Although he was not as prolific as in his first season, Ibrahimovic still contributed to United's success, scoring 7 goals in 17 appearances. However, he suffered another injury in December 2017, which effectively ended his season.

Despite this, Ibrahimovic's impact at United was undeniable. His experience and leadership helped guide the team to two major trophies, and his charismatic personality made him a fan favorite once again. His return to United may have been short-lived, but it was still a memorable chapter in his illustrious career.

Chapter 9
LA Galaxy and MLS Success

In March 2018, Ibrahimovic signed with the LA Galaxy in Major League Soccer (MLS). Many questioned his decision to move to the United States at the age of 36, but he quickly proved his doubters wrong.

In his debut match for the Galaxy, Ibrahimovic scored two goals, including a stunning 40-yard strike that will go down as one of the greatest goals in MLS history. He continued to impress throughout the season, scoring 22 goals in 27 appearances and leading the Galaxy to the playoffs.

Off the field, Ibrahimovic's impact on MLS was equally significant. His star power and charisma helped raise the profile of the league both domestically and internationally. He also became a fan favorite, with his larger-than-life personality and willingness to engage with supporters on social media.

Ibrahimovic's success in MLS paved the way for other high-profile players to join the league, including Wayne Rooney, Bastian Schweinsteiger, and David Beckham (who is now a co-owner of Inter Miami CF).

Overall, Ibrahimovic's time in MLS was a resounding success. He proved that he still had plenty to offer on the field, while also helping to elevate the league's profile and reputation. His legacy in MLS will be remembered for years to come.

Chapter 10
Return To Ac.Milan

AC Milan is one of the most successful football clubs in the world, with a storied history dating back to 1899. The club has won 18 Serie A titles, seven UEFA Champions League titles, and numerous other domestic and international honours.

In recent years, AC Milan has undergone a period of transition, with new ownership and management working to rebuild the team and return it to its former glory. One key signing in this effort was Zlatan Ibrahimovic, who returned to the club in January

2020.

Ibrahimovic's impact on AC Milan was immediate and significant. Despite being 38 years old at the time, he quickly established himself as the team's leader and top scorer. He finished the 2019-20 season with 11 goals in 20 appearances, helping AC Milan to a sixth-place finish in Serie A.

In the 2020-21 season, Ibrahimovic continued to be a key player for AC Milan, scoring 15 goals in 19 appearances before a knee injury sidelined him for several weeks. Despite his absence, AC Milan remained in contention for the Serie A title, thanks in part to the contributions of other key players such as Franck Kessie and Theo Hernandez.

Off the field, Ibrahimovic's influence on AC Milan has been equally significant. His experience and leadership have helped to guide younger players on the team, while his charisma and personality have endeared him to fans around the world.

Overall, Ibrahimovic's return to AC Milan has been a success, both on and off the field. He has helped to re-establish the team as a force to be reckoned with in Serie A and beyond, while also serving as a mentor and role model for younger players. As he continues to age, it remains to be seen how much longer he will be able to contribute at a high level, but his impact on AC Milan will be remembered for years to come.

Chapter 11
Sweeden National Team

Zlatan Ibrahimovic's career with the Sweden national team began in 2001, and he quickly established himself as one of the country's top players. He scored his first international goal in a match against Azerbaijan in 2002, and went on to become Sweden's all-time leading scorer with 62 goals in 116 appearances.

Ibrahimovic played in four UEFA European Championships and two FIFA World Cups with the Sweden national team, and was named the country's Player of the Year on 11 occasions. He was also the captain of the team for several years, and his leadership and experience were invaluable to his teammates.

One of Ibrahimovic's most memorable performances with the Sweden national team came in a match against England in 2012. He scored all four of Sweden's goals in a 4-2 victory, including a stunning overhead kick that was later named the Goal of the Year by FIFA.

Despite his individual success with the Sweden national team, Ibrahimovic was never able to lead the team to a major international trophy. However, his contributions to the team over the years have been significant, and he remains one of the greatest players in Swedish football history.

In recent years, Ibrahimovic has retired from international football, but he continues to support the Sweden national team and has expressed his desire to help develop young players in the country. His legacy with the team will undoubtedly continue to inspire future generations of Swedish footballers.

Chapter 12
Legacy And Impact On Football

Zlatan Ibrahimovic's legacy and impact on football are undeniable. He is widely regarded as one of the greatest players of his generation, and his contributions to both club and international football have been significant.

Throughout his career, Ibrahimovic has been known for his incredible skill, strength, and agility on the pitch. He has scored countless goals and provided numerous assists, thrilling fans around the world with his performances.

But beyond his individual achievements, Ibrahimovic has also had a lasting impact on the teams he has played for. His leadership, experience, and work ethic have inspired his teammates and helped them achieve success on the pitch.

In particular, Ibrahimovic's impact on Swedish football cannot be overstated. He is the country's all-time leading scorer and has been named Player of the Year on multiple occasions. His performances with the national team have been nothing short of legendary, and he remains a hero to fans around the country.

Even in retirement, Ibrahimovic continues to inspire young players and support the development of football in

Sweden. His legacy will undoubtedly continue to shape the sport for years to come, both in Sweden and around the world.

Conclusion

In conclusion, Zlatan Ibrahimovic's impact on football is undeniable. He has left a lasting legacy both on and off the pitch, inspiring fans and players alike with his incredible skill, leadership, and work ethic. From his success with club teams to his legendary performances with the Swedish national team, Ibrahimovic has cemented his place as one of the greatest players of his generation. And even in retirement, he continues to be a positive influence on the sport, supporting its development and inspiring the next generation of players. Ibrahimovic's impact on football will be felt for years to come, and his legacy

will continue to inspire and motivate
fans and players around the world.

Printed in Great Britain
by Amazon

24304039R00020